Valleys Deep 'n' Mountains High

Tracey Odessa Kane

First published 2017
by Rowanvale Books Ltd
The Gate
Keppoch Street
Roath
Cardiff
CF24 3JW
www.rowanvalebooks.com

A CIP catalogue record for this book is available from the British Library.
ISBN: 978-1-911569-31-2

This book is dedicated to my friends and to my adversaries,
both of whom have taught me so much
and have helped to make me a far better me—
for which I am wholeheartedly and eternally grateful.

Contents

Introduction

It is when the infinite—the *other* within our nature, within our hearts, our spirit, our soul—slowly starts to awaken, and begins in earnest to spur us on, that we finally understand, truly begin to perceive the real meaning and truth of life. Of this life. Of our life. The truth that explains, in the most tangible way it knows how, why we are here now, at this very point in history, for such a time as this. The truth which states that in this life... *Anything can happen, and everything is possible.* Valleys Deep one moment, Mountains High the next, and everything in between.

It may not sound like rocket science or feel as grandiose as walking on the moon, but I imagine, nonetheless, that, in the grand scheme of things, this discovery, this simple truth of life and meaning, comes pretty close, no matter what stage of our own life's journey we are on when the revelation happens. For when the foot we have in Heaven and the foot we have on earth begin to walk closely together, ultimate purpose pays a call and we start the process of beginning. We start to become. For, somehow, we categorically begin to understand that everything in our life thus far—for better or for worse, for richer, for poorer, during sickness and in health, everything—has led us to this point, to this very moment. All the lessons, all the hard work, the study, all the mental and physical strain, the emotional investment… everything has brought us here.

And, somehow, we know the winds have changed and that for us our time has come, destiny is upon us. And so, letting go of what has been, we give a nod to the times and trials of preparation and we ready ourselves to go, to begin the definitive climb, to bring together all of our pieces in order that we may be the holistic selves we always hoped it was possible to be. We give ourselves that pep talk, carefully plan our next step, position ourselves so that we can do that which up to this point has only ever been a dream, a heartfelt vision that only we could see.

Now, as that dream starts heading towards its picture-perfect conclusion, the fundamental mountaintop of our life's journey beckons; the culmination of who we are, who we were and who we are hoping to be begins to take shape. Ready for the newest, the most dynamic, imperfection-free version of ourselves to take control of the baton and run with passion and with purpose its leg of the race. The race that is life in all its fullness. Exciting times indeed. The universe wills us to advance forward: courage abides, faith rises, love champions us onwards, tenacity fills our boots, hope carries our hearts and desire takes over the wheel.

The climb itself takes us on this epic, gut-busting, soul-searching, rollercoaster ride, where we come face to face not only with our greatest weaknesses in glorious (or not so glorious) technicolour, but where also we get to witness first-hand our greatest strengths, our gifts, our talents and our abilities, our lasting contribution to the world. Our darkness and our light side by side, working together to reveal who we could be, what we could do if... if only we could wholeheartedly trust in, believe in, have faith in ourselves... and in the experiences of those Valleys Deep 'n' Mountains High that have filled thus far, and no doubt will continue to fill, the pages of our life's story.

"I want you to write your best story."
"But what if I make a mess on the pages?"
"My darling child, that is how you learn."

1. To walk a day in your shoes.

To walk a day in your shoes, what lessons would I learn?
What insights would I gain? What judgements would I overturn?
To walk a day in your shoes, what colours would I see?
What music would I hear? What things would I learn about me?
To walk a day in your shoes, what stories would you have to tell?
What thoughts do you have about life? What do you think of Heaven, of Hell?
To walk a day in your shoes, what path would I walk upon?
What fears would I find, unearth? What dreams would I see, would I stumble on?
To walk a day in your shoes, what pain would I find deep inside?
What hurt would be there in your heart? What would you most want to hide?
To walk a day in your shoes, what would that teach me of grace?
What would it reveal about truth? What would it do to help me run my race?
To walk a day in your shoes, what part of the picture would I see?
What would I understand about pride? What would your faith impart to me?

To walk a day in your shoes, what new
friends would I meet?
What opinions would change, turn around?
What ghosts could I help you defeat?
To walk a day in your shoes, what would I
discover about how you see?
What would I unearth about your
traditions? What would I learn of your
family?
To walk a day in your shoes, what self-
image would your mirror reflect?
What value would I find you place on
yourself? What would truly matter, have
the least effect?

To walk a day in your shoes
What a real privilege it would be,
What a great honour, a wonderful
blessing—
What a way to start to be the Change that
we want to see.

2. Undo you

To live that one perfect day,
remove the battery from the clock.
Leave your phone uncharged,
tell all those thoughts to stop—
Undo that tie, let loose your hair,
put on your old, but comfy jeans.
Pour yourself a coffee,
employ more mindful means.
Dance like a sea
of firecrackers, sing with all
your spirit, heart and soul—
Unleash the beauty of your smile,
let go the need to be in control.
Unset the table—
Post the bills back through the door.
Give the car a day off, put
the compass back in the drawer.
Find a spot to sit in
By a river, under a tree.
Wiggle your toes, read a good book,
allow yourself to simply *be*—

3. More than strangers?

Who are you?
Who am I?
Who are they?
All strangers, until
Life intervenes,
Takes us by the heart,
Encourages us, upon
Friendship to embark.
All strangers, until
One day we meet, and
With warming smile
Genuinely greet,
Not shrouded in all of our
Hurt,
Defeat,
Not claiming to be
Sorted,
Complete!
All strangers, until
We pause,
Reach out,
Let life show us
What it's all about.
Let love inspire us
To stop holding out.
All strangers?

Until...
Who are you?
Who am I?
Who are they?
Friends
And
Family
We haven't yet met.

4. Ploughing the fields.

Partially composed verses, lovingly penned
on crumpled bits of paper, bus tickets,
empty
envelopes, old cigarette packets—
Words forever entwined together, each one
a revelation, a delicacy to slowly ponder,
savour. Such a tantalising flavour; please
can I have some more?
The wordsmith diligently, resolutely
ploughing the fields. Ploughing the fields,
tenacious in each new endeavour—sword
sure.
Excavating the soul's shrouded depths,
unearthing
its treasures. Seeking to uncover its
sorrows,
encounter its pleasures. The rule of thumb
with which it measures—traverses life.
Life thus far uninterrupted...
Not yet fully digested.
Not yet fully known.
Not yet fully discovered.
Not yet fully shown.

Half-written poems,
Aching to breathe—

Captured thoughts
Awaiting reprieve.
Sensibilities, passions,
Airing their views,
Raising their heads
Looking for a muse.
Not fully proven.
Not fully ripe.
Not fully fledged.
Not quite ready for flight.

Half-written poems.
Penned in blood and in ink.
Giving rise to new thinking that could be
gone—in a blink. Impassioned, delightful,
challenging, insightful. Crude, never crass.
A little tempestuous, not defiant. Alas.
Read into that what you will.

Words born for all seasons.
Truth bequeathed for all time.
Its purpose awakens
The spirit, soul and the mind.

5. The Meaning of Life?

Undoubtedly Impossible
Incorrigible, Insane
Breath-taking, Heart-breaking
Bittersweet, Profane,
Captivating Cornucopia
Exquisite Masterpiece
Unwritten, Diabolical
Re-awakening, Deceased,
Incomparable Splendour
Magnificent Lullaby
Generous, Exceptional
Contradiction, Why,
Moving, Unbelievable
Nonsensical, Amusing
Counterproductive, Chaotic
Rudimental, Bruising,
Effervescent, Incandescent
Zealous, Cruel
Gregarious, Intelligent
Foreboding, Crowning-Jewel,
Omnipresent, Sombre
Methodical, Legendary
Unyielding, Captivating
Transparent Mystery,
Harrowing, Rapturous
Reluctant, Unadorned

Uncontainable, Explainable
Outlandish, Scorned,
Monolithic, Insurmountable
Destructive, Justified
Insatiable, Beautiful
Undiscovered, Certified,
Enraging, Melancholic
Subjective, Indistinct
Indignant, Repulsive
All-consuming, Extinct,
Creative, Condescending
Obscure Precipice
Uninviting, Undeserved
Calamity, Abyss,
Unreasonable, Discouraging
Dubious, Aloof
Guarded, Disposable
Illogical, Approved,
Lavish, Unappealing
Irrefutable, Profound
Surreptitious, Cataclysmic
Lost, Found,
Unbridled, Bedazzled
Sumptuous, Strife
Compelling, Experiential
Victorious Life…

6. Planted

Wherever we are planted
We must learn how to grow,
Learn how to make the best of
All we do and do not know.
We must learn how to flourish
Even in a dimming light,
We must learn how to withstand
In times of fight or times of flight.
We must learn how to suffer
In times of drought, of poverty,
We must learn how to share
In times of plenty, prosperity.
We must learn how to cherish
Both the sunshine and the rain,
We must learn how to rise up
When life causes us to fall again.
We must learn how to cultivate
The very best of who we are,
We must learn to love, embrace,
Every fault and every scar.
We must learn to nurture
Every root that leads to good,
We must learn to accept that
Life will always require mud.
We must learn to treasure
And to value this life so,
And wherever we are planted
We must learn how to grow.

7. Let's get naked.

Let's get naked.
Stripped down to the bones
bare. Unrestricted,
unembellished, as nature
intended—totally bare.
Let us peel off
our assumptions, step out
of ignorance and hate.
Let us remove our prejudice.
Take off malice, for
goodness' sake. Let's
get naked. Let us
unleash our birthday suits.
Let us tear off our
misgivings, kick off
those habitual hobnail boots.
Let us divest ourselves all of our
layers. Take indifference
out of our wardrobe.
Let us disregard ill manners.
Embrace the daylight, once unclothed.
Let's get naked. Let us
unmask every face.
Let us undress and ditch
the armour, take the cloak off,
show some grace.
Let us shed all that hinders. Step out

of inequality and violence. Let us
be bold and unattired. Let's get naked—
It's common sense.

8. Public Utterance

I like to write down the things that
you don't say, because
you won't say them and
they need to be said. You'd
agree with me, if only you
could be, would be, quiet. Silent.
Just long enough to let your
voice get a WORD in. To truly
speak, up, out, uninterrupted,
Uninterrupted—
But I see why you mutter so.
Why you utter constantly,
that nonsense—
in public places, always
in public places. I see how
fear rushes in and out…
causing wave after wave of
crushing doubt.
Bombarding you, consuming you —
bit by aching, excruciating bit.
Crashing recklessly, ruthlessly
upon your senses, upon
your soul, like a torrid sea. Defiant,
bitter, resolute in its desire
to completely overwhelm, to

control. To captain and not be
captained, to captain and not
be captained—

When that sea breaks, that bow
breaks too and
you
you fall—
I see how hard you fall, I see
why you think, believe, assume
that you have no choice, no
voice. Life overpowers you.
Life overthrows you. So, you,
you don't speak, not ever. You
don't speak up, out—
Not ever, not ever at all.

9. #Paradox

We see pain and we want to
laugh. We see joy and it
makes us cry. We constantly
make assumptions about others,
and yet—
we feign hope, to help us sleep
at night. We criticise, because
we feel judged. We dish the
dirt to cover our own tracks—
We promote hate because
we are too adult to love. We
choose war because we are frightened
of peace. We divide community
because we find unity intolerable—
We justify our actions in order to hide
our inactions. We paint over
our words to conceal our scars.
We oppose good, because we are
more comfortable with bad—
We ostracise vocation in order
to deny purpose. We find solace
in the dark—
because we are afraid of the
light. We constantly watch
the clock, because we are scared of

spending time. We are scared
of spending time—

We focus on our weaknesses, because
we feel intimidated by our
strengths. We remain silent
because we fear our own
voice. We keep our eyes fixed
on death, so we do not
have to look at life—
We whistle a happy tune,
a controlled but happy
tune, so we cannot hear our soul
dying—

10. Bereft.

Let he who is without
sin—pick the first stone
from the pile. Something sharp,
sturdy, heavy, so it stings
long after it has been thrown—
so it reminds all for a while.
That in this life, upon
this land, we walk the thinnest
line—traverse the path
of Heaven, Hell, whilst spending
our allotted time. And all good people,
in their masses, care not
who you are, have no desire
to read your story—No inclination
to follow your star…
They do not care, nor do they wish
to know, whether you are kind or whether
you
are wise, whether the light of love
shines in your eyes; it matters
not to them that truth is your prize.
To them you are but a face—
A face in a crowd they do not
see, a voice in a riot
they do not hear—a photograph

that's not quite clear. And yet
they'll act as judge, as jury.
In a heartbeat they'll condemn.
Tear your world apart.
Insist that you're not of them.
And one by one they will bend down,
picking stones up off the floor...
forgetting, in a heartbeat,
that to judge another is a sin for sure.
And as he or she casts the first stone,
All of Heaven holds its breath—
for the proof long been suspected dawns;
Mankind of love—it is bereft.

11. Have we sold our own souls?

It's all those questions we don't want to ask,
Fuelled by the things that we don't want to
see,
Aided by all the things that we don't want
to hear,
Fed by the things that we're happy to 'Let
Be'...
It's all those assumptions that we readily
make,
That are weaned on the judgements we
have and we hold,
That are kept by the jailer (A.K.A. our
pride),
Built upon the lies that the devil has told.
It's all those misconceptions we don't want
to face,
Kept alive by the ignorance that is nothing
like bliss,
Cajoled by the determination of wanting to
hide—
As for the Truth, please excuse us, we'll
give that a miss.
It's all those misunderstandings that have
led us astray,

Developed by unchallenged and
entrenched envy and hate,
Entwined in austerities, stories and lies,
Bound up in endless reams of red tape.
It's all those blatant lies that have nailed us,
The ones lived out copiously in plain sight,
The ones that 'Good People' don't want
you to question,
The ones that help you sleep more soundly
at night.
It's all those little white lies that don't matter,
All those omissions, those rewrites, decrees,
All of those *no one else cares, so why
should I bother?*,
All of those *shush, it's our secret, just appease*.
It's all those sins of our Fathers we carry,
All those things we should have better known,
All those lessons unlearned that have tarried,
The liberation from truth that we've
somehow outgrown.
And yet questions remain unasked,
unanswered,
Lies and stories keep being added to, then
retold,
Whilst our heads remain resolutely buried,
And still we don't see that we've sold our
own souls.

12. If Love Is All You Need...

If love is truly all you need
And love will save the day,
And if mountains just ain't high enough
And love will always love us, come what may,
Then why do I see children
For whom no love is found,
Children lost and all alone
Brought forth and left on barren ground?
Do they not need this love
Of which we sing and write?
Do they not need this love?
Would it not protect them in their plight?
And what about the homeless,
The disaffected, hurt, abused,
What about the victims of war—
What of those who did not choose?
Is this love not for them?
Is it just for a select few?
Is this love not for them—
Are they to live without it their whole life
through?
And what of the sick, despised, depressed
What of those tied up in slavery,

What about those riddled with guilt and
shame
What of those living in poverty?
Is this love not for them?
Will it not set them free?
Will this love not make amends?
Will it not change their destiny?
What of those who cannot smile?
What of those who cannot sing?
What of those who have lost their faith—
What of those who have lost everything?
Is this love not for them?
Will it not heal their brokenness?
Will it not help them dream once more,
And help the balance be redressed?
If love is truly all you need
And love will save the day,
Then let us pray to God for more than a
song
And let us learn to love His way.

13. Somebody's Daughter.

I think you said goodbye long
before we had ever said Hello.
Not wanting to waste your time,
you took one look and you said no.
Of course, it wasn't quite that simple—
they said, 'you'd have to take her home.'
And the face I saw that day
is the only one, to me, you've ever shown.
Hatred's a strong word, granted.
And yet—for me it sums it up;
you saw nothing in me that you wanted.
I was but an empty, broken cup.
You didn't hide your disdain
or your frustrations; you let me know,
perfectly well, that since I'd come along
your life was less Heaven—more like Hell.
I was a truth inconvenient.
Evidence for all the world to see.
I was your badge of shame—
with no hope of ever being free.
And although you've tried
to rid yourself, time and time again...

You are stuck with somebody's daughter
Who carries someone else's name!

14. The Sum of All My Fears...

When the whole world turned its back and left you standing there, bare, frightened, alone, lost, hurt and abused... Where did you go? Cruel words, cold stares, everyone sees, but nobody cares. Battered and bruised, broken beyond repair. Fake friends who weren't there... Where did you turn? Heart ripped open, dreams in tatters, so much pain, senses scattered, fingerprint necklace, teeth clattered. So much blood, flesh so sore, so raw, I heard where you'd been and that you saw... Where did you run to? Screaming inside, I'm alive, I'll survive, guts twisting, heart losing will, brain on silent, breathing still, wrecking ball, come take your fill... Where did you go to hide?

What happened to you? I bit my lip, I always hate, despise this bit, questions, assumptions that do not fit, at least it stops you digging, and at least there'll be no twigging ON!?

You'll say you've fallen, I couldn't

conceive, yet it's what you want me to believe, but if you fell you must have fallen hard, been torn apart, along the whole nine yards. Did you know that this was on the cards? Your eyes—they tell me different.

Eyes wide open, I can see how and why you do this to me, without even batting an eye. I'm barely seen and rarely heard, often wistful, deemed absurd, childish, selfish, and noisy too, too demanding, hard on you, the least of these, nothing new, a burden, a weight, a waste of space, it's true!... Where did you disappear? What now? I'll live at least another day, you'll rest in peace because you've had your way. The bruises will fade, the pain will ease, and the blood will clot, the writhing cease. My tears will dry, the sun will set, and tomorrow you'll look at me like we've never met. You'll take me to school and call me pet, whilst telling me not to forget, to keep safe and play nice with all the girls and boys, use my manners, share my toys, try not to make too much noise, do as I'm told, no tricks, no ploys. And as you pat me on the head, you'll smile at me and whisper, *if you tell, you're dead!...* Where do you go from here? This is my mother dear... The Sum of All My Fears.

15. The kid.

I never did manage to tell the kid
everything she needed to hear. I never got
to tell her it was okay to smile, okay to
dream, okay to simply be. Poor kid carried
the weight of the world on her shoulder,
and I carried her. We went everywhere
together; she called me her best friend.
I never got to tell her she was my best
friend too, never got to say goodbye
after he stole me. I'd only known her
a few hours when I first heard her cry;
we'd been whizzing through Piccadilly
Gardens and up and down Tib Street past
the pet shop. She longed for a dog, and
I wished more than anything else in the
entire world that I could get her one. Of
course I couldn't. It was right after she'd
stopped to stare at that little black and
white puppy for the third time in that one
day that I felt the change come over her.
Tangible, definite, an invisible weight that
seemed to engulf her, enslave her deep
within it. That's when I heard her: amidst
the darkness, within the shadows of that
bright summer's day, she began to quietly
sob. You could tell she was holding back,

tell she was desperate not to let herself
be heard. But I heard her; I felt her too.
A tiny little thing, with weight to bear far
too encompassing for a kid of her age. I
longed to wrap my arms around her, to tell
her everything would be okay, to assure
her that she wasn't alone. But in all truth,
what did I know? I couldn't even speak to
the kid, let alone tell her that I understood
whatever it was she was going through.
I didn't understand. I just felt in my own
inanimate way the depth of what she was
feeling. She was alone, alone even with
me. The truth is, all I could do was carry
the kid and, in doing so, momentarily
help, carry her burden. I wish I could
tell her what she needed to hear; I wish
with everything inside me that I could
tell her everything would turn out well…
But I can't. I'm only a bike. Just a purple
fucking bike.

16. SAFE

In this life, within this skin,
upon these streets, are we safe?
Are we seen, can we be heard?
Listen to what I am asking, please—
Are we seen? Can we be heard?
One word—*perhaps*. Do our faces
appear only momentarily, as spots
of rain upon waiting windows? Or as
a bolt of lightning that rips
through the sky and then is
gone? All gone. But not forgotten.
Well, probably forgotten—

Are we safe, cool, sorted, chilled?
At one with everything that encompasses
and dwells within our space. Our
safe space, our walls. Walls upon
walls, upon walls, upon walls of
safe space. Home, and those oh-so-
welcoming
fires, that sit snugly,
resolutely, within these safe walls. These
walls that hear our lullabies and our
profanities, our promises and our lies. Walls
that hear our cries of freedom and see our
shattered lives. Safe walls. Walls upon

which the unseen, unreadable stories of
our lives are printed. Never to be read—
well, not without a good dose of
editing, embellishment, refinement. Not
before we've taken the liberty of
exchanging what we had with what
we wanted. Exchanging who we were for
who we wanted to be. Exchanging how
things were for how we wanted them to be—
Life behind all these safe walls.

But...

The truth is—they're not so safe,
these walls, are they? They breed
tedium, evoke the monsters, gargoyles,
the hidden creatures that live within
us—Safe walls wake up that which
ought to have remained asleep. That
which will inevitably lead us to pick up
our safe walls brick by brick
by brick and begin to throw them at
another, at anyone who even dares
to eyeball the monster now fully
Awake—

Safe walls, full of safe bricks
being heartlessly thrown at strangers.
Strangers we walked by, never stopping
long enough to make friends with.

Safe walls, full of safe bricks
being heartlessly thrown at strangers.
Strangers we walked by, never stopping

Safe walls, full of safe bricks
being heartlessly thrown at strangers.

Safe walls, full of safe bricks

17. No Place Like Home.

There is a secret no one's telling me
About this place called home.
This place where love abides
This place where confidence is grown
This place where acceptance thrives
This place where hope is free to roam…
Except—No, not always.
Sometimes home is a place where
You get called someone's little princess
For all the wrong reasons.
It is a place of secrets and lies,
Pain and torment, fear and betrayal.
Home, a place where you dread
Those familiar footsteps on the stairs,
Panic at the twisting of the handle on your door.
Private property? I wish.
My privates, his property.
Home, full of pungent smells,
His smells as he whispers to you in the night
No sight, no sound, no shred of light.
Black.
Incomprehensible, like his heart.
Home; there is no place like it, or so I thought.
Until it was gone.
Until I was excommunicated from it,

Told never to darken its doors again.
People can't handle the truth.
They don't want to hear it,
They don't like you telling their secrets—
Their dirty, dirty, little secrets.
Private property, his and hers.
And so now the street is all I own;
But I don't own it, do I?
No, the street owns me.
And boy, does it remind me, day in, day out…
Minute by aching minute,
You're mine, it shouts, *I own you*,
You're mine, it screams, *I own YOU!*
You're mine, it laughs, *I own you.*
I'm someone else's princess now.
Now I have new secrets, many daddies.
They cut me and I bleed,
And on me they feed and they feed and they
Question:
Did I ask for this?
Did I have this coming?
Was I born wicked?
Is this truly my lot in life?
What was my crime?
Private.
Answers on a need-to-know basis,
And apparently I don't need to know.
I leave oceans of tears,
Rivers of menstruation,
Pieces of my soul, from time to time,
Along life's alleyways.
It is all I have to show that I was here.
I do exist. For worse or for worse, life is mine.
But, this life is not mine, is it?
Not yesterday, not today—

And I'm guessing, not tomorrow?
I'd rather be home, tucked up in Hell
Than shut out and left to roam.
Ask the streets, if you don't believe me,
These cruel and heartless streets.

There is a secret no one's telling me
About that dream... 'No place like home'.

18. The shadow he casts.

Will you ever truly learn to live, to love,
Will you ever actually look and choose to see
That the pain and fear inside your heart
Stems from what he wanted you to be?
Will you ever once try to understand
The hidden depths of your own soul,
Will you ever find the strength, have courage,
To question that truth to which you cleave,
control?
Will you ever once look in the mirror,
Discover why you are here, at this point
today,
Will you ever dare to acknowledge your
true self?
And the part in your failings that you,
yourself, play.
Will you ever be more than a conqueror?
More than an anti-hero, an opinionated man?
Will you ever once stop and just listen,
Or was listening never part of your plan?
Will you ever seek to consider
The constructive dismissals you so readily
make?
Will you ever endeavour to make amends?
Or are you more at ease with all things
untrue, fake?

Will you ever face up to your own lies,
misgivings?
Will you ever confess to your sin?
Will you ever own up to the fact that
you're wrong;
Will you ever let your healing begin?
Will you ever admit that you've been played?
Or will vested interest ever stand in your
way?
Will you ever be bound all the days of your
life?
To the shadow of a man and all that he
could not say.

19. Her Face

Hers is the face that you'll
never forget, that you always
forget—
That you always block
out. Hers is the heart that you
fought to win. That you love
to break, tear all hope
from within. Hers is the kiss
you could not live without,
will trade for another, will give
a good clout. Hers are the eyes
that spoke to your soul—
Eyes you now like to
blacken, to spit into, control—
Hers is the soul that once
was your mate. Now so easily
neglected, left in the cruel
hands of fate. Hers is the life
that you vowed to cherish—
A life now in tatters, left
so to perish. Now beaten
and broken, beyond all repair—
A tattoo that needs fixing, a cross
she must bear. Hers
is the smile that once stole

your heart, on the face
that you'll never
forget—
hers now the cage, the chains
and the ball, hers the memories
that you did forget.

20. Pitch black

The trouble with hatred? It's ravenous. It devours
a soul from the inside out. From the inside out—
Like a parasite, it enters the body, through an eye
or an ear, or the heart; it cares not how. Even an
arse will do it, just as long as it gets in—
as long as it can begin feasting. Nibbling, touching,
tasting, licking, touching, tasting. Munching, touching,
tasting, crunching, touching, tasting. Gnawing, touching,
tasting. Consumption—
that's what you're left with; one consumed soul. One
crushed spirit. One decaying, embittered body,
crawling, riddled. Now outward-facing, with hatred's
distain. Working steadily, but resolutely, steadily, but
resolutely, until—It starts to bear fruit. Misshapen,

disfigured, rancid, sickly fruit, that tastes like little
pieces of Hell that have been torn off and rammed into
your mouth. Your mouth then nailed shut, until...
your throat closes and you begin to gag, you begin
to squirm, you LOSE—
Sickness, the bastard child of hatred and the ensuing
dance it had with fear. Toxic intoxication, lust, baiting
the need to control, or control, baiting lust, it doesn't
matter anymore who baited who. Nothing matters
anymore—Justification casts a new golden medal.
Arrogance engraves its name on a newly-polished silver
platter; intent vehemently argues the toss, with cause.
Whilst the gates of Hades ardently swing wide open, swing
wide open, to rapturous applause. Hate, the diligent servant,
welcomed home. Standing ovation to all hate has sown...
Poverty, famine, war.
Intolerance, racism, war.
Inequality, greed, war.
Rape, perversion, war.
Death, destruction, war.

21. Return to Sender

Love addressed 'return to sender'
has no time to—grow.
Has no time to lay down
its roots, to bid the heart,
'beat so'. It has no time
to dance the dance that always
will be treasured, no time
to craft those memories…
that never could be measured.
It has no time to photograph
every beautiful, heart-stopping smile.
Has no time to write
those words that make it
all worthwhile—
It has no time to cherish each
And every moment shared, has no
time to reach out and touch,
to show just how much it cared.
It has no time to build a life upon
which impossible dreams
can come true. No time to heal,
to make amends—no time
to always be there for you.

Love addressed 'return to sender'
Has no time to find its

Tracey Odessa Kane

wings; it has no time to set
you free... It has no time
for splendid things—

22. Chopping onions.

Today, darkness obscured the light
yet again. Leaving havoc in its wake.
It tore up roots, ripped off wings,
shook the leaves off all the trees.
And I? I went into the kitchen and
began chopping onions, so I could
hang my head and weep in peace—
No one sees your tears when you
chop onions. No one questions you, they
don't want to know why—your heart
can't breathe any longer, why your mind
can't think in straight lines. Of course,
the darkness knows why you cry. Tips
its hat as it slowly walks on by. Casting its
shadows upon your very spirit, your soul,
shadows over which you have no control.
Fear grips. Tighter and tighter—
Darkness smiles when it sees that you're
Overwhelmed, when it sees that it is
Wearing you down, bit by bit, bit by...
Sickly sweet the look in its casual eyes
As it laughs and calls out your name. As it
Laughs and—
So many lives lost in one single minute.
So much pain that drowns out the sea.
Oceans

Of hurt, mountains of shame. Tsunamis of
grief,
Misery. Tsunamis of grief, misery—
Innocence loses it voice once, forever
It loses its place in the world. Unable
to withstand the darkness, around death's
now grave fingers it curls. And I, I stand in
my kitchen, chopping onions, while the tears
flow on—engulfed by my fears, darkness
heckles and I slowly lose sight of the good.

23. Order, Order.

She may be missing from history's pages
She may be absent from memorial walls,
She may be non-existent in man's tales of
valour
She may be invisible up and down life's
great halls.
She may not have statues carved in her
honour
She may not have trophies and medals
dedicated to her,
She may not have special services of
remembrance
She may not have been given a voice
without a silencer.
She may never be treated as an equal
She may never be in a position of power,
She may never be seen as more than a body
She may never be privy to man's ivory tower.
And yet...
She creates life, she feeds life, she
nurtures
She endows life with meaning, with love,
She tends and she mends and she teaches
She shows life what it's truly made of.
She empowers, she inspires, and she builds
She designs, she discovers, she writes,

She navigates, she buys, and she sells
She moves and she shakes, and she
knows her own rights.
She's courageous, a dynamic risk-taker
She's inventive, a thinker, a sage,
She's revolutionary, she is a leader
She's a testament throughout every age.
And though man has seen fit to paint over
Her endless contributions to the world and
to life,
Though man refuses to let her out of the
corner
He still desires her, longs to make her his
wife.
In conclusion, perhaps that's man's final
solution:
Speak of love, make her a slave to his will,
to his heart,
Enshrine her, turn her into a trinket,
But don't ever once let her play her true part.

24. A law unto themselves

In the privacy of the public sector,
I see people wait their turn, eager
to take their turn—
to light their candles at both ends,
and just burn and burn and burn.
Full of goodwill, good intentions,
wanting to seize their day. Desperate
to be the conquering hero,
desperate to be the change—come
what may!
Desperate to climb that ladder
that will take them to the stars.
Desperate to be all—that matters
in a house made out of cards.

In the privacy of the public sector,
I see people make bad choices—
I see people do their utmost
to silence other people's voices. I see
hunger,
the thirst for power, consume
bit by aching bit. I see the need
to cover up, control, toss all

that's good into a skip. And
all the people they once vowed
to serve and protect now keep
getting in the way. And it becomes less
and less about vocation and more and more
about their pay. This creates a vicious
cycle, a treadmill of epic scale—
A nightmare scenario, a whiter
shade of pale.

Until things reach a tipping point,
where all lose out, that's for sure.
And no one can remember
Who or what the public sector is for.

25. Fifteen minutes later...

We don't underestimate our capabilities, we overestimate them. We convince ourselves we are indispensable, a must-have on a who's who, *people we should know* list. We believe our own press. To the point that it culls any ounce of sense and sensibility—any drop of emotional, intellectual, spiritual intelligence.

Like market traders touting for business, we cry out over and over again. *Buy me, try me, hire me... Buy me, try me, hire me. Buy, try, hire. Buy, try—hire.* Tiresome and belligerent on the senses, to the soul. Prostitution by any other name, only sickly sweet and twice as messy—

Wannabes and has-beens, could have-beens, should have-beens. AWOL in their own flesh, anything but mindful, of time, of place, of space. Of space, of place, of time.

Washed out dreamers, ill-fated
schemers, for whom life's a bitch—if only
they could scratch that itch. And
make it go away. Desire bites!
Desire to be more. Fame—
sold as the only thing worth living for, worth
dying for, worth lying for. Do you
see me now? Polished bright
and shining, all you'll ever need.
Champions' champion—VIP,
we ought to believe. Available for a price.
Motives are anything but pure. Velvet
glove with silver dagger... neither the
answer here nor cure.

26. Earthbound

Sometimes it feels like home is just
a place I heard of once, read about in
a book, a magazine. The home ideal—
Easy to find, always there, no place
like it. Home. Windows, doors, walls, roof.
Windows. Doors. Walls—Roof.
Home. It's where the heart is, is it not?
Until,
without warning, someone or something,
someone or something, sweeps away
the breadcrumbs. Lost—
No way back. Lost. Out on a limb. Lost.
A stranger in a strange world. There is no
Kansas anymore. No welcome mat outside
the door. No familiar smells, no succour.
Nothing. In that moment you become
nothing.
A round peg that has no chance
whatsoever
of fitting in a round hole—
Empty. Homeless. Alone. Wandering,
constantly
wondering who or what swept those
breadcrumbs
away; no clue. Who. What? None.

Wandering, always wondering, along life's beautiful,
heart-breaking, mesmerising, soul-destroying road.

Down that road, I carried with me what I thought
was a box full of hopes and dreams. I never
opened it, never dared to—I just assumed
it was full.
Assumed they were all mine to keep, to do with
as I wished, to do with as I wished—
Assumption made a fool out of me. I treasured
an empty box. Some days it feels like I've lost
the plot—Do you ever feel like that?
Like one minute, life is taking your very
breath away for all the right reasons, and the next
minute, for all the wrong reasons—

Earthbound. No wings. No roots. No hopes. No
dreams. Just one recurring thought, just one—
There is No place like home.

27. All for the want of...

For the want of power we sold the sky,
For the want of a kingdom we took an eye.
For the want of a medal we created war,
For the want of land we broke every law.
For the want of treasure we raped the earth,
For the want of selection we controlled birth.
For the want of renown we bought the vote,
For the want of revenge we slit the throat.
For the want of bias we made a loophole,
For the want of money we sold our souls.
For the want of impiety ourselves we defiled,
For the want of depravity we molested the
child.
For the want of safety we built nuclear arms,
For the want of sacrifice we nailed holy palms.
For the want of oil we bled the world dry,
For the want of peace we turned a blind
eye.
For the want of youth 'n' beauty we grew
embryos,
For the want of fun we snorted crap up our
nose.
For the want of a servant we built a ship,
For the want of obedience we branded a whip.
For the want of racism and hatred we wore
a hood,

For the want of evil we destroyed all that
was good.
For the want of power we sold the sky,
For the want of a kingdom we took an eye.

28. Doubt

Sometimes I think that I have the answers
To life and to all that it means
I think I understand the whats and the
wherefores
I think I get the hope and the love and the
dreams
But then, always, then, like a shadow, a
thought,
A doubt, creeps into my heart
And I remember that in truth I know
nothing—
Not how life will end nor did start
So many questions bubble deeply inside me
So many thoughts that just go on and on
So many pictures shaped just like a jigsaw
So many lyrics, but the music is gone

Sometimes I think that I have the answers
To life and to all that it means
I think I get the plan, the big picture
I think I understand the grand scheme
But then, always, then, like a river
Comes doubt that just drowns out my mind
And as much as I look, seek to find it
It's like all at once I've gone blind

And all the things that I once saw so clearly
And all the things that I once understood
Now all seem muddled, all empty,
Like a forest that's minus the wood

Sometimes I think that I have the answers
To life and to all that it means
I think I've got it sussed out, that I've
nailed it
Coz the truth fits me like old comfy jeans
But then, always, then, like a missile
Comes the doubt that will blow me apart
Come the thoughts that look set to
consume me
Comes the fear like a poisonous dart
Is there any real rhyme or real reason
To this life and the struggles we face?
Is there any true hope or great purpose?
Will it all end here or in some other place?

Sometimes I think that I have the answers
To life and to all that it means
But then, always, then, like a chainsaw…
Doubt rips in, tears life apart at the seams.

29. You Do The Maths

Too many excuses:
If, buts and whys.
Too little endeavour,
So much compromise—
Much disappointment,
Shedloads of regret.
Weighty expectations
Dreams sold,
Hope sublet.
Fear born without reason,
Doubt running amuck.
Denial sings sweetly—
Whilst hate pushes its luck.
Love no longer believed in.
Kindness dead in the water
The price of a coffee
For a son or a daughter.
Soulless the journey,
Corrupt the path.
So many excuses.
You do the maths.

30. Valleys Deep 'n' Mountains High

Through valleys deep, and over mountains
high
Through winter snow, under summer sky,
Amidst April showers and autumn's glow
Under God's great Heaven, above Hell's
fires below.

Through good and bad days, through
wrong and right
Through foreboding darkness, embraced
by the light,
Amidst timely intervention, when things all
go wrong
Under the weight of trial, when the heart
is free as song.

Through wondrous adventure, entrenched
in deepest regret
Through sadness and through sorrow,
when every need's been met,
Amidst thoughts and ponderings, when it's
all work, no play
Under a splendid rainbow, Another Day
Someday.

Through bitter betrayal, on the road to
find one's self
Through seasons ever-changing, in times
of poverty and wealth,
Amidst reflection's encounter, blow, a
friendship that lasts all time
Under true love's protection, when peace
is hard to find.

Through every dream and every vision,
when your head aches from it all,
Through every scheme and unkept
promise, when you receive that timely call,
Amidst the gathering clouds of heartache,
when laughter has no end
Under thrill of great endeavour, when your
soul does bend.

Through every pressing moment, when
the day is done
Through every act of unforgiveness, when
your race is run,
Amidst the forest bluebells, with a sad and
heavy heart
Under the mystery, life's journey, at the
end and at the start.

Love is ours to treasure, hope is ours to
keep
Faith has not a measure; grace does not
end nor sleep,
And if we deem to cherish stranger, foe
and friend
Life will be ours in all its fullness, and joy
will know no end.

31. Me First.

If hope could lead to love,
and love led us to
peace, could we not meet
it then? With open arms
allow faith to move, increase?
And what of the sisters—kindness,
compassion—must we ever turn
them away? All because someone
once stole our trust; now, we no longer
seize the day. Who counts the cost
of our grave choice to give up in this
way? The young and old,
the silent voice, all the good people
of today? All these questions
I cannot decipher; I don't know how
to respond to apathy. But
when I think of hope that leads
to love and love that leads to peace,
One thing I know above all else:
Hope must first be born in—me.

32. #Metathesiophobia

I never even realised that I was resistant
to change. Until
change tried to change me—
Can you believe? Change tried to change
me… No,
neither could I. I mean, I enjoy change as
much as
the next person; I welcome it. But there's
a time—
And a place, and a time and a place… Is
there not?
And, well, without deliberately intending
to be as blunt as a brick, this is not the time
or the place—
I mean, come on, which clown thought
now would
be a good time? Who told change I had
nothing
better to do? Was it you? I swear there'll
be Hell to pay
when I find out. Whoever it was made me
look like
a fool, and now change thinks I'm part of
the bloody
resistance and I'm NOT! I'm not, I—I just
need
to prepare myself, that's all, it's no big

deal. It's not
an issue. We don't need to dissect it or
create a hashtag
and start trending it on social media—
#purpose #notready #changeresistance
#metathesiophobia
I'm #okay ☺
I'm just not quite ready, that's all—
Give me a break, cut me some slack and get
back to me... next week maybe? Hang on,
I'm
away next week. Tell you what, make it
the week
after that, hey? Just remembered—I'm
dog-sitting
that week, our kid's away. How about next
month?
I know, I'll check my diary and get back to
you
ASAP and we'll pencil something in—
I say pencil, because you know how things
have a tendency to creep up on you, then
the
plans you made—
Well, you know what happens to them.
You have
to change them—rearrange them. Nobody
likes
rearranging things, do they?

I'll call you later, I promise, I'm just off to
get
a tattoo. What's my tattoo going to be?
It's a picture of Ghandi and the words
'Be the Change'. Awesome, right?

33. My Dearest Child.

My dearest child,
I'm writing with the hope that one day you
will understand
That the life you see all around you is not
as I wished or as I planned—
I find it so hard to quantify all that has
happened on my watch,
Things I was far too busy to attend to
whilst moving my career up a notch.
The wars that were nothing to me but a
video game, because they were on TV,
The violence that I tolerated, because it
was towards someone else's family.
All the animals that have become extinct, I
cared not for their plight,
I never thought once about preservation,
about doing what was right.
I knew of the little children who were
starving to death, each and every day,
Little children with no clean water, who
had lost the will to play.
I understood that they had no book, no
education, I knew they were often bought
and sold,
I knew that some of them were soldiers,

without a hope of ever growing old—
I knew about global warming, the
poisons we'd pumped into the seas, the
atmosphere,
I knew all about the dangers of trident, I
planned to recycle more next year...
I watched as capitalism killed decency,
I stood by as racists threw their hatred
about,
I kept my head down in the face of
oppression, I turned away from those who
cried out.
I saw the way that women and girls were
treated, the sheer lack of equality,
I saw all the vulgarity, the filth that they
had to deal with, but in the end, it didn't
bother me.
I saw the welfare state become the must-
hit target, as the vulnerable were further
ostracised,
I watched as people queued for miles
at foodbanks, but even to this I was
desensitised.
I watched as young men were driven to
suicide, a way out of this life being their
only goal,
I saw how they struggled to find their
place, how mentally chains wrapped
around, crushed their spirit, mind and
their soul.
I watched as all the libraries were closed,
as the NHS died a violent death,
I saw human rights go up in flames, and
yet I did not feel bereft—
I watched as once-banned drugs became

quite legal, I watched as abortion replaced
the need for the pill,
I saw what the church has done to God,
how it's now God who foots that bill.
I didn't do the things that I could have
done, let alone the things I should have
done,
I didn't care about pollution, I never once
looked for a solution,
It was all about me, me, me—
I didn't think about your children, nor
about the kind of world that they would be
born into;
It seems I didn't think at all about what I
would be leaving behind for you.
And now the penny is finally dropping, the
revelations plain to see,
All the things I didn't care about, to you,
child, become this parent's heartless
legacy.

34. Embers

Cascading thoughts upon the windows
Church ringing loud its bells,
Sands of time are shifting
The truth the story sells. Now,
Lost but not forgotten,
In a world where no one cares,
Discarded, laid to waste
One table, so many chairs.
Through a door that leads to nowhere
We all scrambled to get through,
Leaving all that's good behind us
As well as all we never knew.
Though the solace of peace lingers
As the embers in a fire,
We don't recognise the offer
We are unaware that cometh the hour...
Those embers will breathe one final
breath, then
Peace forever will leave these shores.
And in our life, minus its meaning,
Fear will dig in ever deeper its cruel and
vile claws.

35. The Road to Restoration

Tell love to grow once more,
Ask hope to wake,
Implore courage to arise,
Beg grace not to forsake.
Apologise to inequality,
Put things right with truth,
Employ restoration,
Show healing some real proof.
Make amends with kindness,
To acceptance, open the door,
Rebalance justice's scale,
Pick beauty up off the floor.
Invite peace to indulge us,
Request that trust come home,
Encourage faith to believe again,
Get forgiveness on the phone.
For today we must remember
What fear and hatred cost,
Where ignorance can lead us,
The sheer and utter loss.
Today we must pause, be still,
We must say a silent prayer,
Remember those we failed to protect,

Though they were in our care.
Today we must acknowledge
The lessons we fail to learn,
From the missing generations
Who never got to take their turn.
Today we must remember
The stain on history,
We must face the legacy of bitterness,
Recognise what will set us free.
And as all heads are bowed,
And the silence floods our weary soul,
Let us humbly begin
To give change the leading role.

36. MIND

If I had my time over again, I would say, "Brother,
Please don't leave. Sit down with me, let us talk
a while, for I see how your heart does grieve—
let me lift that great burden from off your shoulders, let me take the strain; let me care
for you amidst your brokenness, allow me to understand—your pain. It is true, I'm not
a healer, and I haven't always been there, I haven't
always been patient, I haven't always been fair.
And when life saw fit to take us down two separate roads, I didn't stop and turn around—I
didn't stop and turn around, I don't know why; perhaps Heaven knows?
Winter in and summer out, mountains high 'n'
valleys deep, I kept on walking, kept right on
walking—I had no promises to keep. I never

saw you, never heard you, in my heart,
my soul, my mind, I never pondered what
life
had dealt you, I had no questions, cruel or
kind—
You were the past from which I had
escaped, that book that I had burned,
you were the song I'd long since forgotten,
the lesson I had spurned—and yet
you always remained my brother, bound by
blood, by life eternally, bone of my bone,
flesh
of my flesh, reflected in the mirror back at
me...

I'm so sorry that I hurt you. I'm so sorry I
let
you down, so sorry I had no faith in you—
I'm so sorry I did not turn around."

If I had my time over again, I would say,
"Brother,
please don't leave, sit down with me, let
us talk
a while, dear brother, just please don't you—
leave."

37. Take Time To Read Your Story.

Take time to read your story.
The message was spoken loud and clear—
So, withdrawing from the world,
I found a place where I could hear.
All the things my heart was saying,
All the songs my soul did sing,
All the poetry written on my pages,
All the thoughts my mind was experiencing.
And as I turned each page before me
I began to get this sense of awe,
As I began to see, to understand,
What I had been made, created for.
I began to see within me
Such possibilities untold,
I began to see, to realise
What it is I have and hold.
For there so deep within me
In each atom, vessel, my core,
Were the life-cells of my creator
So, too, his truth, his plans, and so much more.
All at once I had a revelation:

That my story's in my hands,
And the fulfilment of each page
Is determined by my vision, plans.
I felt so scared, if I am honest—
What if I blow it, make a mess?
What if I miss the point completely?
What if I fail to achieve, redress?
All the dreams I have within me,
All the things that have gone wrong,
All the questions, all the answers
All the silence, every song.
What if I leave the real me wanting?
What if I simply walk away?
What if I turn my back on destiny?
What if I fail to LOVE each day?
Take time to read your story
The message was spoken loud and clear;
So, withdrawing from the world,
I choose to unmask each lie, my fears...

38. Mindfully Yours

Should I be bold and wake up the moon
and the stars,
To tell them of my plight?
Should I bid the sun to listen?
Do I have to face the fact that I will not
win this fight?
Should I ask the wind to grant me its
courage?
Ask the rain to shower my cause with
great hope?
Should I ask the ocean for a little of its
tenacity?
Do I simply have to let go, cut the rope?
Should I ask the mountains for solace?
Do I go into the desert, find a sand dune
and hide?
Should I speak to old Mother Nature?
Am I just wilful, soaked in my pride?
Should I speak to the trees to gain
understanding?
Maybe it's the lilies in the valleys whom I
need to ask.
Should I enquire what the honey bees
think?
Or am I simply avoiding the task?
Should I wait till the summer is over?

Perhaps winter's a much better time;
Should I paint God a glorious picture?
Do I have to admit that this one life is
mine?
What if I break or misuse it?
What if I stumble and fall?
What if I set fire to it, or lose it,
What if I make a mess of it all?
Should I be trusted with a gift that's so
precious?
Shouldn't there be some instructions, one
call to a friend?
What if I take the wrong path?
What if I bring it to an untimely end?
Should I be bold and wake up the moon
and the stars
To tell them of my plight,
Or should I just take a deep breath and
dive in—
Have faith enough to believe that it will all
turn out right?

39. Not one grain.

Captivated by my own dreams,
enslaved by their charms—
I imagine other, different worlds. I
perceive other choices, see new,
unchartered seas. Roads, paths,
upon which no sole of any
soul, has ever stepped. I hear
different kinds of voices
clearly—
Colours blend, dance with joy,
Because there, in those other worlds
there, they are free. Entirely
free to be—
Unjudged, unrestricted, untamed,
at utter peace. Cups full to
overflowing. Each a rose unlike
any other. Each an unwritten story.
Each a tender mystery. Beloved,
bright, beautiful. All things, bright,
beautiful. Each comfortable in
their own unthreatening skin—
Unambiguous. Without contempt,
content, deservedly content. I
understand completely the
possibility, the probability, that
created all of this—No Fear.

No Fear—the artist.
No Fear—the architect.
No Fear—the builder.
No Fear…
Can you imagine a world with
no fear? None, not one grain.
Breath-taking, for all the
Right reasons—
I see that world. I dream
that dream.

40. 'Da fidei quae fidei sunt'

When darkness looms at your door
And tries to pick at the lock,
When emptiness fills your soul
And each demon throws a heavier rock.
When courage is but a memory
And hope a childish thought,
When fears become insistent
And help cannot be sought.
When the screaming gets more frequent
And the bells toll, call your name,
When the chills rip through your bones
And you feel like you're going insane.
When you feel you're at Hell's mercy
And the shadows are drawing near,
When you feel like giving up
And you'd rather end it here.

Hold on tight and don't give up
For there's a few things that I've learned:
The sun always comes after the rain;
The tables all get the chance to be turned.
Good always overcomes evil,
Experience is always a prize,

Trials help us to grow stronger,
Tests help us to become gentle and wise.
And lies teach us discernment
And greed shows us how to give,
And all that was meant to cause us harm
Helps us to challenge, amend, truly live.
And if we have faith, just a little,
And if we just trust for one day,
And if we forgive and show grace
Peace will find us, come what may.

41. Free At Last...

I feel an inner sense of calling to another
place in time
Where I will unearth the mystery of this
soul and why it's mine,
Where I will look and will determine the
real me I never knew
Where I will open up my mind to all that's
good, that's decent, true.

I sense a gentle but real awakening of my
spirit, my inner self
A picture of a time long since forgotten,
a revelation creating wholeness, bringing
health,
And as I turn towards it and embrace it,
joy consumes and fills my heart
Splendour opens up my eyes, inspiration
fans into flame the spark.

And with courage and with boldness, I
open every window, every door
I open my ears and truly listen; I see all
along, the real picture was so much more,
And as the canvas grows ever brighter and
the words ring crystal clear,

The truth ignites my senses and I lose all
sense of fear.

I see there before me, ready to teach me
all she knows,
The childlike me I banished so long ago,
the best of me that truth exposed.
Taking my hand, she leads me forwards,
to a place I've been before
To a place that feels like home, but
somehow home and so much more.

And waiting there to warmly greet us is a
quill, some ink, an empty book
Our treasured memories, our experiences,
a map that shows the route we took,
Time to talk, to become friends, possibility
beyond all expectation,
Wisdom's gift to comprehend and great
hope in our reclamation.

And with trust gained, demons defeated,
with insight gleaned into what could be,
With understanding weighed, recollections
tallied, the plan returned to A, not B,
We take the call, ready and willing; we see
the way, the purpose too,
With pen in hand and paper willing, with
love enough to see it through.

We turn the page and journey onwards,
together once more, as in times long since
past
Ready to live the life God gave us,
together now as one, and Free At Last.

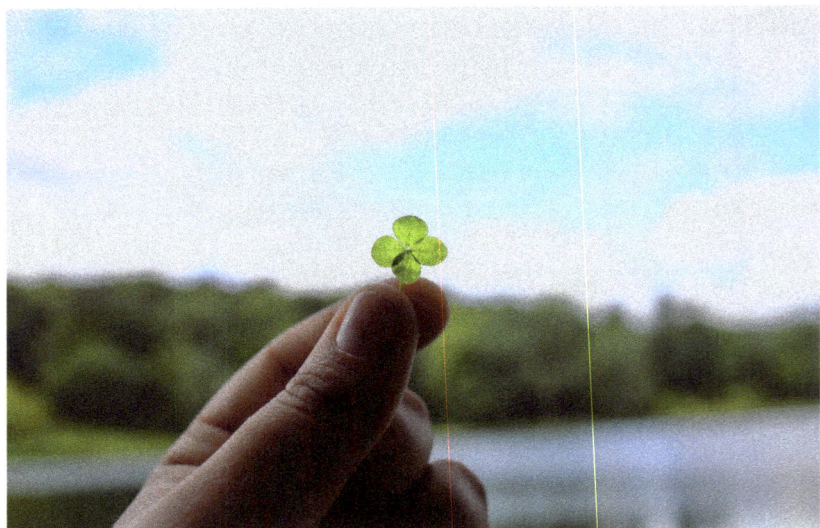

42. #7daysaweek.

Monday is just the beginning...
The first day of the rest of our lives,
The promise of hope sent to guide us,
The chance that finally arrives.
It's the day packed with great expectation,
It's the day we envisioned, way back when,
The day we began to embrace, to love life,
our journey,
The day God called and we said, "Yes," and
"Amen".

Tuesday is willing and able...
To unleash its potential, its might,
It's ready to equip and to guide us,
Ready to help us to fight the good fight.
It's willing to help us to reach and aspire,
To be so much more than we dreamt we
could be,
It's waiting to deliver its gifts,
Waiting to help us find the truth that will
free.

Wednesday's got the 'WOW' factor...
If you are mindful of its ways,
If you totally embrace its unique position,

And the intrinsic role it duly plays.
It's the day things start to come together,
It's the day we give it another try,
It's the day we stop making excuses,
The day we truly believe we can fly.

Thursday's got it going on…
It can turn your week around,
It can remind you why you started,
Why you think your vision's sound.
It can chase away your doubts and fears,
It can put paid to procrastination's games,
It can help you to create something quite special,
Ensure that your passions never grow cold, are tamed.

Friday's all about thanking goodness…
For all the week did have 'n' hold,
For the experience, the purpose, the challenge,
The strength, the courage to be bold.
It's the day that we kick our shoes off,
The day we ponder all that has been,
The day we dance just because we can,
The day we once more start to dream.

Saturdays refresh, restore your soul…
They give you time to pause, reflect,
They make space for you to write that book,
To take long walks, with life reconnect.
They present you with the time to simply be,
The time to try something brand-new,
They grant space for you to chill out with good friends,

They allow experience to talk, to share
with you.

Sunday's the day to embrace your why...
It's the day to seek and find,
It's the day you're equipped to travel
onwards,
The day you give thanks, then leave the
past week behind.
It's the day that God reminds us
How life, how love, is truly meant to be;
It's the day we accept, take up the
challenge,
To run our race with faith and seize our
destiny.

43.
#LoveYourOwnFace

#LiveYourOwnDream
#TakeYourOwnPath
#SpeakYourOwnWords
#DoYourOwnMaths
#DanceYourOwnDance
#SingYourOwnSong
#WriteYourOwnStory
#RightYourOwnWrongs
#ShineYourOwnLight
#PlayYourOwnAce
#BeYourOwnHero
#SetYourOwnPace
#ComposeYourOwnMelody
#CaptainYourOwnShip
#DiscoverYourOwnRiches
#LoosenYourOwnGrip
#ForgeYourOwnDestiny
#CultivateYourOwnWill
#SeizeYourOwnMoment
#PayYourOwnBill
#UnleashYourOwnTalents
#FreeYourOwnMind
#LoveYourOwnBody

#ToYourselfBeKind
#ReachForYourOwnStar
#TrustInYourself
#BeYourOwnAnswer
#UnderstandYourOwnWealth
#ListenToYourOwnHeart
#SetFreeYourOwnSoul
#HaveFaithInYourOwnGifts
#BelieveInYouTakeControl
#EmbraceYourOwnLessons
#LoveYourOwnFace
#PlanYourOwnFuture
#RunYourOwnRace

44. Seeds of Greatness...

Lying within the human spirit, its soul,
seeds of greatness await the time
When every man and every woman will
release that spark that is divine.

But for the moment they lie sleeping, ill at
ease with why they are,
Ill at ease with their great purpose, ill at
ease with the bright morning star.

And I'm not sure what will stir, wake them,
I'm not even sure they will yet wake,
Preferring still their mighty slumber, and
all things material, unreal, fake.

I think man fears its own potential; I think
man fears what he could be,
I think man fears its sleeping giant, I think
man fears its destiny.

And I don't know what will alleviate fear—
the drugs and alcohol didn't work too well—
Nor did the mindlessly wasted lives that

reflected nothing of Heaven, just scenes
from Hell.

Perhaps a glimpse of why this matters, a
look into eternity,
A look at a Saviour's Truth, His passion, a
look at what together we could achieve.

Lying within the human spirit, its soul,
seeds of greatness await the time
When every man and every woman will
release that spark that is divine.

But for the moment, they're contented to
shun today, embrace the past,
For the time being they see no reason not
to make this moment last.

And I'm not sure what will disturb them;
children suffering, dying needlessly,
People being bought and sold, hatred,
wars and famine, excruciating poverty?

I think they look but they see nothing, I
think they listen but do not hear,
I think they're aware but see no
consequence; all they know is darkness,
fear.

And I don't know what will wake them,
what will cause their hearts to feel,
What will cause in them reaction, what will
convince them all this is Real.

Perhaps a visitor from the future, with

proof that without change this does not
end well,
Or maybe someone from the pages of
history, who woke, saw the light, but then
did not tell.

I have no final thoughts, conclusion, only
ears that hear and eyes that see,
The seeds of greatness awaiting the time
when We Wake and Seize Our Destiny.

45. Transformation

Seasons change
Circumstances change
People change.
I've changed, you've changed,
Change happens.
Change—
It's part of life,
The mechanics,
The oil that lubricates,
Pushing us forward,
Enabling us,
Equipping us,
Teasing all of that…
Possibility
Potential
Purpose
Greatness
Out of us.
Change… it
Comes whether you are
Ready
Or
Not!
It's unyielding, unapologetic,
Resolute,

Canny,
Brash.
The foolish
Try to outrun it,
The stubborn
Try to resist it,
The fearful
Try to hide from it,
The angry
Categorically blame it,
The lonely
Resent it,
The bold
Delight in it,
The learned
Aspire to it,
The wise
Encourage it,
The young
Drink it in,
The old
Give thanks for it,
The creative
Utilise it,
The brave
Fully Embrace It.
Change...
How do you
Take yours?

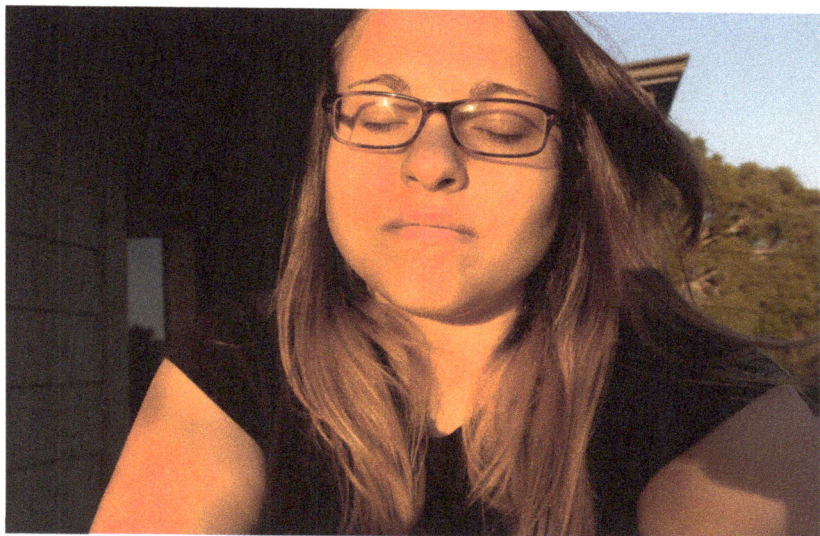

46. "Talitha koum!"

Every night before I go to sleep I ask for answers,
answers to prayers. And every morning I wake up and find more.
More tests, more trials—more tests, more trials, more...
Sent not to discourage or alarm me, but to help me
to find my own answers, to be my own solution, to be
my own healer, the author of my own life's story, the artist
ready to paint upon my own canvas. I needed a physician;
He taught me how to cure my own ails, taught me how to slow
down, to be more grateful about life and living. To be still,
be silent, comfortable in my own space. To connect with the breath
and the life and the beauty all around me, within me.
To breathe deeply, to breathe deeper still— to practise
compassionate mindfulness with self and

with others. To meditate,
to ponder—to be a beginner. I needed to
understand, to learn
how to perceive goodness, grace,
faithfulness, mercy; He taught me
how to seek, how to see not through the
frailty of
my human eyes, but through the holistic
eyes of my heart,
my spirit, my soul. I wanted to discover
new places, go
where no one had ever gone before; He
taught me how
to hold my pen and write. How to chart
those uncharted waters,
without and within. How to carve out a
new trail, to transcend
the here and now, to connect with all that
was, all that is
and all that is to come. How to find the
real voice within me and
set it free. Devotedly, unequivocally and
utterly free.
I wanted to forget my past—He taught me
how to embrace it.
How to learn from it, to fully experience all
that it had
to teach me. He showed me how my past
had bequeathed to me
fruit, fruit grown in total darkness, in my
darkest times, in those dark,
dark places. Wonderful fruits of the spirit:
love, joy, peace,
forbearance, kindness, goodness,
faithfulness, gentleness and

self-control. Good things out of bad, new
truths, revelation.
Promises, foundations on which I now
stand...

Faith—Hope—Love—Forgiveness—Grace.

He taught me how to take all that was
meant to harm me
and fashion it into something new,
something beautiful,
something worthy, something of Him. Love
unconditional.

I asked to be changed, to be turned into
someone else, to be turned
into someone new, someone beautiful,
valued, good. He held
a mirror up to me and He slowly but surely
helped me to see
everything that He sees, everything He
created, everything He loves.
He helped me understand that I am
unique, fearfully and wonderfully
made, purposed for such a time as this.
Valued, loved, beautiful.

Every night I ask Him for answers to my
prayers; every morning
He whispers, "Talitha koum!"

47. #LifeLessons

I've learned that hatred will never mend a
broken heart
That fear will never overcome the dark,
That self-pity will not inspire faith
That guilt will never help you run your
race.
I've learned that mountains can be real
friends
And that pain is oft the blessing that God
sends,
I've learned that enemies are what make
you stronger, bold
And that to grow we need both hot and
cold.
That the things you force, well, they are
sure to fail;
That you must carve yourself out a unique
trail,
That you must believe in wonders yet
unseen
That you must boldly go and fully dare to
dream.
I've learned that meditation soothes the
aching soul
And that you're closer than you dare to

think to your life's goal.
I've learned that tears bring growth, as does the rain,
And the course of true love is very rarely plain-sailed.
That laughter wards off falsehood, wards off pride
That amongst the crowd is often where we hide.
I've learned that friends, they come and then they go,
And that angels stay and help you as you grow.
That tomorrow may never even come—
That if it does, your journey may be done.
I've learned that singing gives you wings and helps you fly
And that to live your life, you're going to have to die.
That patience is a virtue and a gift
That love's the only glue to truly mend a rift.
I've learned that happiness is priceless, can't be bought,
And that manners are a choice; they can't be taught.
That truth is something not everyone can take
That many prefer copies and things unreal, fake.
I've learned you shouldn't believe everything you hear
And black and white doesn't make the picture clear.
That all too often a lie is easier to swallow

That there's no justice, just a procedure
that's pointless, hollow.
I've learned that bitterness will kill you
before you're dead
And that the battle's at its fiercest in your
head.
That the wind repeats everything you say…
That pain will very rarely go away.
I've learned that the map you have to
follow is often wrong
And that most days you'll feel like you
don't belong.
That on junk you'll ever live, be ever fed
That often perilous is the path that you
must tread.
I've learned a smile can get you further
than a car
And that you're tall enough to reach the
highest star.
That you can have your cake and eat it too
That there's no one else as wonderful
(quirky, crazy, beautiful, unique, funny,
charming, special,
sensible, fearless, gorgeous, talented,
brave, lovely, etc., etc.)
as You!
I've learned to err is human, to forgive
divine
And that as for the content of my life's
story? That choice is mine.
That this poem will run and run and run
Because my life has only just begun.
But for now, ponder, relax, sit back,
unwind.
And come tomorrow, expect another line…

48. Harmonious Cohabitation

In search of hope, I travelled
over land and over sea—mountains
high, valleys deep, further than
the eye could see. I met so many
people; we talked and talked
and talked. We shared food, we
shared our hearts—we sat;
often, we walked. We listened
with loving kindness to each other's
fears, concerns. We listened to
each other's experiences and stories,
aware we all needed to learn—
How to mindfully ask our questions,
speak truth to power with one voice.
How to express clearly the rudimentals,
Face people who have no choice.
We reimagined life and living—
Dreamt of a more equal and
inclusive society. We put forth
our proposals—regarding collaborative
community. Education shared all
its concerns; re-education stated its case.
So too did sustainable development.

micro-finance spoke with wisdom, grace.
The arts welcomed our endeavours,
explained
where in this new world they would fit,
their concern being the lack of man's
aspirations and not letting apathy
renew its grip. It was then
that innovation revealed its
hand. Motivation was given the floor.
Inspiration gave a holistic view. Efficiency
vowed that it would do more—
Discord promised to back off; fear
agreed to bow out. Anger said
it would hang up its gloves—
Disease packed its case and
checked out.

And life, it gave the biggest cheer
as hope came into view. Harmonious
cohabitation, now more than a dream:
it is the means, and the end too.

49. Love Wins

Love happens
To us,
Through us,
With
Or
Without
Our permission.
It waits not
For us to be at ease with it,
Ready for it,
Looking for it;
It comes and it sweeps us
Clean off our feet.
It does not wait
For us its charms to greet,
With open arms,
Sweating palms.
It doesn't respond
To our fears,
Our woes,
Our maybes, noes,
It's unyielding in
Its lovelorn quest,
Its rudimental,
Effervescent,

Childlike zest;
It will not rest.
It pours extravagantly,
Abundantly,
Its loving balms.
Until it consumes,
Drinks in your heart,
Its path to chart,
Till death do part,
Until it takes
Your very
Breath away,
By which time
You have no choice
But to let it stay—
Love Wins.

50. Write Your Best Story

Behold the dreamer
Who seizes the dream,
Hats off to the thanksgivers
Who understand all life means.
Champion the carebringer
Who heals and restores,
Acknowledge the teacher
Who does not seek applause.
Give thanks to the child
Who gently reminds,
Praise all the thinkers
Who open our minds.
Show some respect and listen
To those with experience to share,
Offer kindness, thanksgiving,
To those who work to make all things
equal and fair.
Be humble to those
Who toil through the night,
Give thanks to those
Who fight the good fight.
Be gracious to those
Who take time to learn,

Say thank you to those
Who patiently wait their turn.
Always bless and pray for
Both the friend and the foe,
Be ever prepared
To learn and to grow.
Write your best story
With tenacity, grace,
Live the life that you dream of.
Run with passion your race.

Author Profile

Tracey Odessa Kane's lifelong passion, writing, emerged during her childhood. The youngest child in a forbidding family situation, writing became her most trusted ally, her saviour; it gave her solace and allowed her to think and to say all of those things that her everyday life wouldn't allow her to voice. Her experience of being a young mother had a profound influence on her and her writing. Having always dreamt of writing books that could help people like her who had been forced to suffer imposed silence, she seized the motivation she'd gained from having a son. She wanted above all for people to know they were not alone, that they were loved, valued, had worth and purpose, in spite of the hand life may have initially dealt them. And so Kane's quest began. For the past thirty years, she has dedicated her life to helping those whom for whatever reason cannot help themselves. She's volunteered to help her Church and community, and has worked within charity and education sectors.

Her desire to help others to communicate has always played a huge part in this, so much so that she has received awards both locally and nationally. Although she left school at a young age with no qualifications, she loves to learn and has furthered her education, forming links with not only Sheffield and Chester University, but with a wide and varied range of training providers, including The Institute of Leadership and Management and The Coaching Academy. It is Kane's belief that everyone matters and has the absolute right not only to be heard, but to be educated, equipped, empowered and encouraged, to be treated justly with fairness and equality, and it is to this cause that she dedicates her life and her writing.

Publisher Information

Rowanvale Books provides publishing services to independent authors, writers and poets all over the globe. We deliver a personal, honest and efficient service that allows authors to see their work published, while remaining in control of the process and retaining their creativity. By making publishing services available to authors in a cost-effective and ethical way, we at Rowanvale Books hope to ensure that the local, national and international community benefits from a steady stream of good quality literature.

For more information about us, our authors or our publications, please get in touch.

www.rowanvalebooks.com
info@rowanvalebooks.com

Rowanvale Books

www.ingramcontent.com/pod-product-compliance
Lightning Source LLC
Chambersburg PA
CBHW042339040426
42448CB00019B/3335